The Aquinas Lecture, 1959

METAPHYSICS
AND
IDEOLOGY

Under the Auspices of the Aristotelian Society
of Marquette University

by

Wm. OLIVER MARTIN, Ph.D.

MARQUETTE UNIVERSITY PRESS
MILWAUKEE
1959

Library of Congress Catalog Card Number: **59-9870**

© Copyright 1959
By The Aristotelian Society
Of Marquette University

To Grace

Prefatory

The Aristotelian Society of Marquette University each year invites a scholar to deliver a lecture in honor of St. Thomas Aquinas. Customarily delivered on a Sunday close to March 7, the feast day of the society's patron saint, the lectures are called the Aquinas lectures.

In 1959 the Aquinas lecture "Metaphysics and Ideology" was delivered on March 8 in the Peter A. Brooks Memorial Union of Marquette University by Dr. Wm. Oliver Martin, professor of philosophy, University of Rhode Island.

Born in Columbus, Ohio, September 15, 1903, Dr. Martin received his A.B. degree from Wittenberg College in 1925, his M.A. degree from Ohio State University in 1929, and his Ph.D. from Harvard in 1934.

Dr. Martin joined the faculty of Ohio University in 1936 and remained there until accepting his present position in

February, 1949. He is currently chairman of the department of philosophy.

In 1952-54 Dr. Martin was secretary of the Metaphysical Society of America. He is also a member of the American Philosophical Association, the Associataion for Realistic Philosophy, the Philosophy of Education Society, the Religious Education Association, and the Academy of Political Science.

While on a sabbatical during the academic year 1957-58 Dr. Martin completed a study of comparative education and curricula in European universities.

It was while on a Ford Fellowship for Advancement of Education in 1952-53 that he conducted the research and organized much of the material which was published in his book, *The Order and Integration of Knowledge* (Ann Arbor: University of Michigan Press, 1957). In addition, Dr. Martin publishes regularly in *The Review of Metaphysics*.

To his writings the Aristotelian Society has the pleasure of adding *Metaphysics and Ideology*.

Foreword

During the academic year of 1957-1958, I visited many universities on the continent, and in Britain and Ireland. Previously, with William Brickman of New York University leading a group of educators, I had visited the classrooms of secondary schools in many European countries. Always my special interest was in the status and health of philosophy *as an academic subject*. Depending upon the location, and allowing for some exceptions, I found the patient not well. The same observation could be made with respect to the United States.

But observation is not the same as scientific diagnosis; it is only the occasion for the latter, and points up the urgency of proper therapy, the beginning of which might well be the distinction implied in the title of this essay. To him in whose name these lectures are given, the distinction would not be wholly foreign—only its contemporary relevance in institutions of higher learning. And so, one cannot help but imagine St. Thomas returning to the University of Paris today—perhaps walking up Rue de Vaugirard and crossing Boulevard St. Michel to enter the Sorbonne. What he would see dominating the *Place*, of course, is a large statue of August Comte. The scene mirrors in a sort of molecular form much of the history of the West in modern times.

Metaphysics and Ideology

INTRODUCTION

There are philosophers and anti-philosophers. Some anti-philosophers are ideologists. The exact relation between
ideology and philosophy, or, more speci-
fically, metaphysics, has perhaps never
been adequately formulated. In this brief
essay we intend to speak to the problem.

In what follows, "metaphysics" and
the general term "philosophy" may or may
not be equated, the specific meaning to
be understood in context. "Ontology" will
include metaphysics and/or some kinds of
theological propositions. The term "ideology" means essentially what Karl Mannheim refers to when he says that ideology
is a "quest for reality," but one that is
relevant only for practice; it is "an instru-
ment for dealing with life-situations."[1]
This use of the term is continuous with

that of Henry D. Aiken when he says that "the nineteenth-century philosophers became involved in a gigantic task of ideological and cultural reconstruction which precluded the very possibility of doing philosophy in the time-honored 'rational' and 'objective' ways which had prevailed in Western philosophy since the time of Plato and Aristotle."[2] From the standpoint of ideology, he continues, "the whole history of ideas in the modern age may be regarded as a history of the progressive breakdown of the medieval Christian synthesis which had been most powerfully articulated in the *Summas* of Thomas Aqinas . . ."[3] Furthermore, the ideologists were far more concerned "in raising practical doubts concerning traditional religious and moral attitudes than with the bare description of the pervasive traits of being, as such."[4]

A problem is posed. Since ideologies do often seem to deal with being, or "reality," how can one distinguish metaphysics from ideology? Today, unfortunately, the confusion is so widespread that both in professional journals and in popular writings the terms "ideology" and "metaphysics" (or "philosophy") are often used interchangeably, almost as synonyms. Since part of the essence of ideological criticism is that metaphysics is not a science, we shall ask and answer the question as to what would be the distinguishing marks of metaphysics if it were a science. Then we shall ask what, if anything, best meets the criteria, make some applications to the history of philosophy, and finally sharpen the contrast between metaphysics and ideology.

FOUR CRITERIA OF METAPHYSICS
AS A SCIENCE

Either metaphysics is a kind of knowledge, or it is not. A kind of knowledge that is a science is composed of propositions. Concepts help to make up the entities which are propositions. Concepts and propositions are kinds of mental beings, *ens rationis.* Hence, a kind of knowledge is a kind of mental being. As a kind of being it has a nature, an "essence." And so, metaphysics must have a nature; otherwise it could not *be* something. It is to be noted that although we have expressed this in realistic language, the thesis is not peculiar to realism. Even if one were to take concepts and propositions as kinds of real beings, nevertheless a kind of knowledge such as metaphysics would have to have a nature. Otherwise it could not be *a* kind of knowledge.

If this is true, then like any kind of knowledge its nature is marked out by its subject matter and method. Since method is partly determined by subject matter, it is subject matter that is most important. The peculiar subject matter of metaphysics is being *qua* being, or is that of the nature of ultimate causes. It is in this manner that metaphysics is distinguished not only from other theoretical sciences, but also from practical sciences. This manner of distinguishing not only has historical precedent, but will not likely be denied except in terms such that metaphysics as a kind of knowledge is also denied.

If metaphysics is a science, then as any other science, it must have a history and also be systematic. In addition, as a basic theoretical science, it must be both autonomous and adequate, i.e., it must account not only for other forms of knowledge but also for itself. The latter it will do through the help of epistemology. But the problem of the nature of truth and knowledge is peculiarly related to metaphysics.

These criteria are the distinguishing marks of metaphysics looking at it from "the outside." Metaphysics as truth, as a kind of knowledge, is "seen" to be true from the "inside"—perhaps the only way any kind of knowledge is understood. In other words, these criteria do not constitute the truth of metaphysics, but rather are the characteristics by which, from the outside, one may recognize true metaphysics from among systems making competing truth claims. Just as one laughs because he is human, and not conversely, so a metaphysics has these characteristics, i.e., satisfies these criteria, because it is true, and not conversely. Put in another way, from the standpoint of the order of the being of truth a metaphysics is true (relative to others) because it *is* true. In the order of knowledge a metaphysics is recognized as true, in part, because it has the marks represented by the four criteria.

The criterion of autonomy. If metaphysics is a basic theoretical science, then it is autonomous. This means, first, that metaphysics has its own data, its own kind of evidence, its own formal object. Second, it is an experiential, though not experimental, science. Metaphysics has its own concepts and protocol propositions derived from experience. "Valence" is a concept of chemistry, "substance" is a metaphysical concept. Neither one is a concept of, say, mathematics. And the one is quite as experientially grounded as the other. In short, "substance" is not a postulated "construct" related, in some manner or other, to non-metaphysical data as evidence. Third, if metaphysics is an experiential science having its own data, and hence autonomous, then it follows that no other science or kind of knowledge is constitutive of metaphysics. A kind of knowledge may be instrumental to metaphysics, but the nature of the evidence which would be sufficient to prove a non-metaphysical (and also, non-theological) proposition would not be sufficient to prove or disprove a metaphysical proposition. If this is denied, then it must also be denied that metaphysics has any data or evidence of its own. If this is the case, then there is no formal object which makes possible the definition of metaphysics, and hence, whatever it may be, it is then no longer a science. To illustrate. Both mathematics and a posi-

tive science, say, physics, have objects
which define and delimit them. Mathematics is instrumental to the knowledge
which is physics, but it is not constitutive
of it; i.e., mathematical data do not constitute evidence which proves anything in
physics. To deny this would be equiva-
lent to the reduction of physics to mathematics. Similarly, the positive sciences
may be instrumental to metaphysics. But
if the evidence or the data of positive science determine the truth of metaphysical
propositions, then metaphysics is reduced
to positive science and ceases to be a science in itself.

When metaphysics lacks a formal object, and hence ceases to be an autonomous science, it does not become nothing.
Rather, it becomes a formal system to be
used as a means for some human purpose.
The inversion carries over even with respect to truth. Instead of a system prov-
ing satisfactory because it is true, it becomes "true" because of its usefulness as

a means of serving some human purpose—
anything from peace of mind to social ad-
justment to social revolution. A metaphysics becomes an ideology, a "Weltans-
chauung," or a "personal philosophy."
Concepts no longer have a foundation in
things; they have a foundation only in human purposes. Concepts are now mere
"constructs," personal or institutional.
They are "ideas." First principles become
"postulates." The order of being is reduced
to the order of knowing, and knowing is
reduced to making or doing. The history
of philosophy becomes the "history of
ideas"; in other words, really the history
of ideology.

The criterion of continuity. One of the
distinguishing marks of metaphysics as a
science is that it is systematic. What that
means we shall presently consider. First,
however, let us ask what it means to say
that metaphysics as systematic must also
have the mark of continuity. It seems that
truth is not given to man all at once; it

must be struggled for. Hence, there must be a history of the development of man's search for metaphysical truth. This history will include more than just the history of metaphysics as a science. But in both histories we should be able to find permanence and change.

If so, then we may say that in the development of metaphysics as a science some principles will be discovered to be true and will be held as such through whatever changes the system may undergo. Examples of such principles would be: The existence of any contingent being necessarily depends upon some other actually existing being; If potential being is actualized it must be actualized by actual being. It should be observed that for the moment the relevance of the examples does not depend upon the principles being true. If one were to uphold a certain type of naturalism as the true metaphysical system, such naturalism being based upon principles which contradict the aforementioned principles, i.e., based upon the primacy of potency over act, then these principles would have to remain as a partial, permanent unity which establishes continuity through the development of that kind of naturalism. Whether a system be naturalistic or non-naturalistic, if it makes a knowledge claim, then it has a nature, an essence, which makes it *what* it is. Whatever may be the principles which constitute its nature, which make it *what* it is, these principles cannot change in truth-value without the system itself being destroyed.

Those who would reduce the history of philosophy to the history of ideas would say that if all this is so, then the science of metaphysics cannot have a history. For if the first principles are true, then they are true and do not change. If there is no change, then they have no history; and if there is no history, then there can be no such thing as continuity. Hence, our demonstration involves a contradiction. The only way out is to admit the change which is history, give up the notion of metaphysics as a systematic science, and reinterpret the history of philosophy (at least, metaphysics) as the history of ideas.

This kind of criticism has only the appearance of plausibility. In fact it is merely a statement of the consequences of denying metaphysics as knowledge. What one is really saying is something like this. If we assume change to be absolute in the order of being, then in the order of knowledge there can be no metaphysical knowledge. And if there can be no metaphysical knowledge, it is foolish to seek it. However, from the beginning there have been those who have sought for metaphysical truth. Now, if we do not have any systematic truth which they have discovered, we do have, as an historical fact, their *ideas*. And since the men who created the ideas influence each other in such creation, we can have the history of such influence, together with a history of the uses to which men put the ideas in various societies and cultures.

Of course, formally this kind of reasoning is excellent, and we would insist on its validity. It shows one of the logical consequences of absolutizing change. The question is concerning the relevance of the reasoning. If the absolutizing of change is not to be taken as a truth, then the whole "argument" reduces to nothing but an ideological weapon used in the attempt to destroy man's rational nature. It is not, then, something to be rationally answered, but a corruption to be exposed. On the other hand, if the absolutizing of change is considered to be a metaphysical truth, then the argument is self-contradictory, for metaphysical truth is assumed in order to show that there is none.

In order that metaphysics be knowledge all that is required is that change be not absolute, that in some sense there is permanence as well as change in metaphysical development. Let us see what this "sense" may be by considering the various kinds of change which may be found in a science.

There are those changes which are extrinsic to the being of any science, e.g., changes in symbolic expression—in language and style. The intrinsic changes are those of the ideas or concepts, the propositions, and the system as a whole.

A concept or idea may have a permanent and a changing aspect. The concept of man may include "rational," "sentient," "living," "corporeal substance." These elements are fixed and unchangeable in one sense. For if any one of these elements should be lacking there would be a "substantial" change and the concept of man would be destroyed. (If one should object to this conception of man as being wrong or inadequate, such objection would be relevant only to the choice of the example we have used, not to the thesis for the sake of which we have chosen the example.) Each of the elements, in turn, have elements, since they, too, are concepts. If there is substantial change, and a concept is destroyed, it comes about directly or indirectly. The destruction would be direct if man was conceived as pure spirit, thus eliminating the element called "corporeal substance." The destruction would be indirect if the *name* of one of the elements was retained but the concept which is the element is destroyed in some manner. For example, in some forms of naturalism "rational" refers simply to a form of bodily behavior. In this case a new concept of man is formed—"man$_2$" instead of "man$_1$." Now, from the standpoint of either concept the other must be judged wholly, not merely relatively, inadequate. When these concepts are used to form propositions, then such propositions become respectively incompatible. And when the propositions become constituents of "systems," then they become mutually contradictory in such a manner that both cannot have a knowledge-claim.

Either "man_1" or "man_2" has no foundation in the "nature of things." One must
be a "fiction." Existentially or denotative-
ly the two "systems" are not talking about
the same thing.

It is to be observed that at this stage
the problem is still philosophical. The
"revolution" is *within* philosophy; it is not
as yet the overthrow of philosophy in favor of ideology, which is anti-philosophy.
There is no overthrowing of metaphysical
knowledge as such. Rather, there is simply a conflict of knowledge-claims in a
rather radical way. The problem is to be
solved by further study. Since the possibility of metaphysical knowledge and truth
is admitted, the issue must finally be resolved in favor of one position rather than
another. And, needless to say, resolved on
the basis of evidence.

In the development of philosophy substantial change in concepts can be helpful.
From a purely ideal standpoint one might
think that it would have been desirable

if thinkers could have gotten on the right track—whatever it is—immediately at the beginning of philosophical thought. But it is history, not the possible or desirable, that exists and that we must consider. It seems to be man's lot to be forced to understand truth in terms of error, and hence the history of errors becomes integral to the history of philosophy.

Substantial change in metaphysical concepts is not a sufficient condition for ideology, for ideology must be understood in terms of the use which is made of the concepts. To illustrate with the example given, ideology (and hence, anti-philosophy) would arise if one were to argue as follows: The concept "man," was useful in the process of organizing current impressions and interests of certain past ages, i.e., such interests as those of Heaven and Hell, the eternal perpetuating of one-self, etc. Now the interests of contemporary man are in this world, not the next, and hence the urgency of secularizing religion demands more useful concepts than the traditional ones. For this reason the concept "man$_2$" is "truer" today.

The implications of such an "argument" should be noted. *The conflict between truth and error within philosophy—as a consequence of substantial changes in concepts—now becomes a conflict of ideologies within institutions and societies.* However such conflicts are "solved," rational argument, knowledge, and truth on any other than the instrumental level become quite irrelevant. Since there is no philosophy, there can be no history of philosophy, only the history of ideas. The substantial change of philosophical concepts now becomes a substantial change of the concept of philosophy itself. Instead of "philosophy$_1$," which is now destroyed, we now have "philosophy$_2$," which is ideology.

The other kind of change in concepts or ideas is "relative" in the order of development. Analogically one might speak of potentiality and actuality in connection with such development. A concept such as "electricity" might grow from relative inadequacy to relative adequacy. At one time a clear idea only potentially, it develops in clarity, looking at it in the history of physics. In the history of chemistry one could trace the development of the idea of "valence." It can now reasonably be said that a beginning student of chemistry, who encounters the notion of valence early in his first textbook, cannot have an adequate understanding of the concept until sometime later when he understands physical chemistry. Here, the individual student recapitulates, in his learning, the development that took place in the order of knowledge, the development of chemistry. Similarly, metaphysical concepts may be said to develop. Unless we are doomed to skepticism we can say that relative to the 5th century B.C., the concept "reason" has more meaning for us, and is better understood by us, today. Similarly, in the case of the notion of being in the Aristotle-Aquinas development. For Aristotle, a composite thing in nature was to be understood metaphysically in terms of form and matter, and being is thought of in terms of form. For St. Thomas, being is thought of primarily in terms of *esse,* the act of existence, which constitutes the unity of a composite being. Something has been added; the notion of being has changed, not in any substantial manner, however, for being is still form relative to matter. The change is in the primacy of existence relative to essence. Substantial change in the concept of being would only occur if, as in some kinds of modern existentialism, existence is thought of as something excluding, or incompatible with, essence. Again, the concept of God may be said to have grown and developed in the theistic tradition in such a manner that even on the level of reason alone we now know more of God than did Aristotle. Of course, if, with Whitehead, one conceives of God as potential being whose eminent reality is made by the evolution of natural things in the world, then growth in idea ceases; there is a substantial change conceptually, for the old idea is completely destroyed.

And now we come to change in connection with propositions and truth. It is propositions that are the elements of metaphysics as a science. Concepts are constituents of propositions. Truth, or a knowledge-claim, attaches to propositions. Concepts are relatively adequate or inadequate and, in a strict sense, are not "true." For the purpose of analysis let us consider a proposition, e.g., "Socrates was a courageous man," and see how the truth of it may be said to change and not change.

A. One may understand the proposition, but neither know it to be true nor believe it to be true. In the learning stage of this person there does not seem to be evidence for the proposition. Perhaps Socrates was a fool.

B. One may believe the proposition and yet not know it to be true. There may be little understanding or awareness of the evidence. This might well be the case of the beginning student in philosophy who, in either relative humility or indifference, accepts the word of the teacher.

C. A person, having some minimum understanding, may know the proposition to be true. It may be the same student in a more advanced stage.

D. The same person, after years of experience as a teacher, may know the proposition to be true, and with increasing understanding and awareness of the evidence.

Now, truth has its subjective and objective aspects. Assuming for the purpose of illustration that the proposition is not false, then we can say that from the standpoint of the *being* of the truth the proposition was always *actually* true in all of the four cases. In A, from the standpoint of knowing, the proposition was *potentially* true or false. In B, from the standpoint of knowing, the proposition was potentially true. In C and D, the proposition which, in its being, was always actually true now also becomes actually true from the standpoint of knowing.

Objectively, truth is being; subjectively, truth is a becoming. From the standpoint of being, the truth of a proposition cannot change, although from the standpoint of knowing, one may not actually know it is true. For a person *may* have a true proposition without knowing it to be true just as he may have a cancerous tumor without knowing it to be cancerous. This was the case of the student who believed (i.e., he *had* the proposition) that Socrates was a courageous man even though he did not as yet know it. From the standpoint of knowing, in the becoming of truth from potentiality to actuality, one discovers the truth he may already have believed. This is what a person means when he says: "I now better realize what I already knew."

It is a problem of pedagogy, a problem in the order of learning and teaching, to devise means whereby the actual truth as being of a proposition is appropriated, grasped by the mind, so that a person actually knows the proposition as true. The aim is to make actual subjectively what was already actual objectively. But the locus of this "making" must not be misunderstood. The function of knowing is to discover the truth, not create it. If this is denied, then the act of knowing the truth becomes identical with the act of creating the world the true proposition is about. But such a view eliminates knowing, for under the guise of dealing with the problem of the art of knowing one reduces knowing to art, i.e., to making or creating.

To summarize: (1) There can be no change in the being of the truth of a proposition; once true, always true, and once false, always false. (2) In knowing there can be an absolute or substantial change from true to false, and conversely. (3) There is also relative change in the order of knowing, from the potential true or false to the actual true or false.

In terms of this analysis of truth and change an interpretation can be given to the notion of "partially true." Also, we may note that there is another kind of change that is relevant to the notion of "partially true." A proposition may *be* false, yet *thought* to be true. But, when proper qualifications are added, we may then have a proposition that both is and is thought to be true. An example would be the Boyles and Charles law of gases which, originally, *was* false and yet thought to be true. Later the law had to be changed—requiring, of course, a different proposition—in order to take account of high pressure ranges. This example illustrates another way in which truth may change, may "grow."

The analysis given may be applied to metaphysical propositions. Since this is rather obvious, for the purpose of illustration we may better use a philosophical proposition indirectly resting upon metaphysics, one which we may find in Plato: "It is better to suffer injustice than to commit it." A person may believe it to be true, but have little understanding of its evidence, and not know it is true. And yet, if the proposition is true, there is a sense in which he *has* the truth without knowing it. This is a potentially dangerous situation, for, since he does not know it to be true, he may later, for some reason, believe it to be false. He may have "discovered" that only a sucker continues to suffer injustice, and that if one is to be a free individual and not a slave he must seek and obtain sufficient power in order that, with respect to injustice, he may be on the giving rather than the receiving end. At this point there is a substantial change in the subjective aspect of truth.

Still later, as the result of study, it may
dawn upon him that after all the proposition is actually true. Here, again, there
is a substantial change in knowing, for
now he does not merely believe the proposition, but to some degree knows it.
With further study the proposition becomes increasingly understood and known.
He sees it now in terms of fuller evidence.
A person can actually grow spiritually
while suffering. In fact, many have.
However, the committing of injustice cor-
rupts the person. The change here is relative, a becoming from potential known
truth to actual known truth. At the same
time he now knows that the being of the
truth of the proposition was not only true
for Plato but is true now, and that in the
future no conceivable set of circumstances
can alter the truth. The truth of the proposition is timeless; and if God exists, it is
eternal.

The criterion of system. It may not be
possible to state the complete meaning of

"system" such that it is adequate for any and all experiential, rational sciences. But a minimum meaning can be given. Additional qualifications can then be made for any particular science which requires them because of the nature of its subject matter.

1) No system in any experiential, rational science can be complete in its truth. In this sense—but not just in any sense—the whole truth is not something to be had at any one time, but something to be asymptotically approached. This recognition of incompleteness is sometimes expressed by saying that a system must be "open" and not "closed." It should be added, as a word of caution, that a system, just as a human mind, should be open only at one end, not both ends. Otherwise, as in some interpretations of "open-mindedness," there are no principles, no system—in fact, no knowledge at all.

2) A system must be coherent. Coherence means that a system is formally

non-contradictory, and also that it is consistent with the data that constitutes its subject matter. Any science will be more or less systematic because human knowledge is always in process of development. A perfect system is an ideal to be attained, and hence is not accurately descriptive of anything. But it can be said that any science is systematic to the degree that it is coherent.

3) In any systematic, experiential science a distinction must be made between what is essential and what is non-essential in it. In practice it may be difficult to find the locus of each. The first principles of a science would certainly constitute part of its essence. This means that if the first principles should be found to be false, then a substantial change would be caused such that the system would be destroyed. On the other hand, there may be propositions within a system for which there is some experiential evidence, and yet which do not themselves flow from the first prin-

ciples. That is, they are not really implied
by the first principles, and yet are not incompatible with them. If, later, for some
reason, one of these propositions is
denied, there is only relative change in the
system because nothing essential has been
affected. And yet such change may make
for greater coherence. For example, a first
principle in moderate realism is that act
accounts for potency. The denial of this
destroys the whole system. On the other
hand, consider the proposition: "Accidents
always actually inhere in any substance."
This may be denied, for some good reason,
in favor of a proposition containing "potentially inhere" rather than "actually inhere." And if certain truths about the Holy
Eucharist are admitted, then it could plausibly be argued that such change in propositions produces increased coherence.

A critic might point out that the distinction between what is essential and non-
essential in a system of science is irrelevant
with respect to the contemporary view of

the nature of physical science. If the word "essence" is to be used at all, then what is essential to a system, say, physics, is not a group of propositions called "first principles," but rather a set of rules of procedure which constitutes the method. From the standpoint of this "operational" view no proposition of physical science has any privileged status. Therefore, our medieval-sounding distinctions are irrelevant for contemporary physical scientists, irrelevant to what they actually do.

In answer we may point out that, from the standpoint of the history of science, it is highly questionable whether scientists have ever in fact limited themselves to such a sophisticated view of physical science. Be that as it may, we would rather point out the element of truth in the critic's objection and interpret it. From the standpoint of truth, physical science is part of natural science, which in turn is the same as "the philosophy of nature" properly understood. To understand the science of "natures" both the contributions of positive science and the ontological is necessary. The "ontological" refers to the metaphysical and/or the theological. Although full understanding of natural things requires the ontological, nevertheless it is possible to abstract from it. When this is done, then by definition we have positive science. Such abstraction is not only possible, but may be desirable for certain human purposes provided one understands the price that is paid. Even though such abstraction may never be complete, to the degree that it is, a physical science such as, say, physics is transformed from a science into an art, for a shift has taken place from subject matter to method, and from truth to utility. The rules of operational procedure become a practical means to a utilitarian end, namely, that of control as well as that of prediction. The concern has changed from that of truth about physical fact to that of the relative usefulness of a hypothesis.

To return to the critic's objection, what he is saying is that to the extent to which physics becomes an art and not a science the distinctions we made are not relevant. We would insist upon this, too. But it would also follow that to the extent to which physics became a *system* of truths, then the distinction between the essential and non-essential would be relevant.

Finally, we may observe that the distinction in question is relevant in the case of metaphysics as a science, whatever may be the answer for physical science. The kind of abstraction which makes possible positive science is not a corruption in itself. The corruption occurs only when it is not understood what has been done. However, since it is impossible for metaphysics to be a positive science, the attempt to make it so would be identical with its corruption. Metaphysics would cease to be systematic, theoretical, or science. It would become an art; it would be ideology.

The criterion of adequacy. A concept is relatively adequate to the degree that it re-presents formally its object. A system of knowledge that is a science may be said to be relatively adequate to the degree that it re-presents formally the subject matter that defines it. We shall see that there are special demands made upon metaphysics, because of its nature, that are not made upon any other science.

1) To be adequate, a system of metaphysics must directly or indirectly be able to account for other kinds of knowledge, or at least allow for their possibility. This means that the nature of, and order of, knowledge cannot be understood without metaphysical presuppositions. This is rather obvious if different kinds of knowledge are concerned with different modes or aspects of being. For example, to give a rather unlikely case, if a metaphysics would not allow for the notion of "matter," then it could not account for the nature of physics or chemistry. Or, if it al-

lowed for matter but not for the notion of "living," then it could not account for the existence of, say, biological science. In such cases a metaphysics would be absolutely, and not merely relatively, inadequate.

2) To be adequate, a system of metaphysics must directly or indirectly be able to account for itself as a kind of knowledge. No other kind of knowledge either explains itself or other kinds of knowledge. The nature of history as knowledge is not an historical problem, nor is the nature of physical science a physical science problem. Again, although there is a history of physical science, history does not account for physical science as a kind of knowledge. However, directly or indirectly metaphysical knowledge will be required in order to understand the nature of metaphysics. A metaphysics that cannot meet this criterion is absolutely inadequate. For example, if a metaphysics only allows for instrumental intelligence in man, then that

metaphysics would be inadequate because the knowledge that man is limited to instrumental intelligence could never be known merely by such intelligence.

3) For any scientific system to be what it is, it is necessary for some truth to exist and be known. This may seem to be obvious and hardly worth mentioning, for it is impossible to have a scientific system without some truths. However, what we are calling attention to is what might be called the "existential criterion of adequacy." What is merely possible does not yet exist. Metaphysics cannot be a science if it is merely possible and does not exist. Therefore, one cannot say that metaphysical truth is an "ideal" to which one or more systems are approximations, but that no metaphysical system is really true, i.e., contains some true propositions. One would have to have some evidence to say this. Such evidence would itself be metaphysical, and hence such a thesis would be self-contradictory. Such a thesis is re-

ally an elliptical way of denying metaphysical truth. For if metaphysical truth
is always "ideal," then the so-called metaphysics that *exists* is not really *that* at all.
It is *really* ideology.

What is "ideal" is the "whole truth,"
or "all the truth," and this is the case for
any experiential science. But if for metaphysics to *be*, some truth must be known,
then since truth can only be had by persons it follows that some people have what
metaphysical truth there is. This fact has
implications for those who are "seekers"
and who insist upon "open inquiry." It
would mean that they should go to those
who profess to have metaphysical truth,
and then work on from there. This is the
first step in open inquiry. Having found
metaphysics as a science the next step in
open inquiry would be to seek more or
fuller truth *within* the system. But it is
pure cynicism and a species of dishonesty
to insist on "seeking" and "open inquiry"
when what one really means is that meta-

physical truth is wholly ideal, and hence no one has it, or that it can't be found anyway, and if any one pretends to have it he is dogmatic.

4) A metaphysical system is adequate to the degree that it can account for and absorb all metaphysical truth known in the past and that will be known in the future. This is adequacy in principle. Since no systematic science can ever be totally complete at any given time, metaphysics can never *in fact* be adequate, meaning finished and complete. Can some new truth discovered in the future overthrow a system of metaphysics and make it absolutely inadequate in principle? Such a possibility must be allowed for, and for three reasons. First, it is implied by the fact that a metaphysical system must not be closed at both ends, but must be open at one end. Second, if the possibility were not allowed, a metaphysical system could never be disproved. But if this is theoretically impossible, then the system could only be aban-

doned because no longer useful. Meta-physics would be reduced to ideology. Third, such a possibility must be allowed for because metaphysics is on the level of reason and not faith. However, granted all this, the responsibility of the critic of a metaphysical system, i.e., one who would say the system can never be adequate in principle, is that of showing that there is some truth *now existing* which contradicts the essence of the system in question. It is not enough to show that the proponents of the system are not aware of the truth; nor is it enough to show that some truth which is not incompatible with the system has not been sufficiently emphasized in the past.

Perhaps it may be well to consider what kinds of metaphysical criticisms are possible, for all criticism is concerned with the criterion of adequacy in some sense or other. A metaphysics may be criticized on metaphysical grounds. Or, one may attempt to do so on non-metaphysical grounds. Let us consider the first alternative. A metaphysics may be shown to be formally contradictory. Such criticism is either relative or absolute. If relative, then the system may be improved. If absolute, and the criticism is justified, then the system is destroyed, meaning that it is essentially false. What does it mean to say that the criticism is justified? First, the critic must present one or more propositions which contradict the system in question. Second, these propositions must have a substantial amount of evidence for them in order that they may have a truth-claim. Third, although it is not immediately necessary that the critic present an alternative metaphysical system of which these propositions are parts, it is necessary that the propositions be parts of an actual or potential system. Otherwise they would be but a few propositions dangling in a metaphysical vacuum and having no implications whatever. The substantial evidence required would be lacking. If the critic cannot identify himself with any actual system of metaphysics, then the few propositions he uses should, if true, cause a coagulation such that a system would gradually be formed.

The other alternative for a critic would be to criticize any metaphysics as inadequate simply because there is no such thing as metaphysical truth. But such denial must be stated in one or more propositions of some kind of knowledge for which a truth-claim is made. What kind of knowledge is this? It cannot be metaphysics, for that would involve a self-contradiction. It cannot be epistemology, for that rests upon metaphysical presuppositions. It cannot be one of the positive sciences—psychological, social, or physical for insofar as their autonomy lies in their abstraction from the ontological they cannot be used as evidence against all ontological truth. (This requires some explanation, and is given elsewhere.)[5]

But may not metaphysical truth be

denied in the name of theology? Now, it is possible for a given metaphysical proposition to be incompatible with a specific theological proposition. However, this fact is not relevant to the issue. Without getting involved in the whole problem of the relation of faith to reason, we may sharpen the issue in the following manner. Either theology is concerned with truths of revelation, or it is not. If not, then there is no problem. For either it becomes, then, the same as natural theology, or it is a religious philosophy which, in any case, presupposes metaphysical propositions. On the other hand, if theology is concerned with truths of revelation, then one cannot *think* about these without assuming metaphysical truths. For what can one *use* to think with? The positive sciences? Hardly. Logic? But, unless logic is reduced to arbitrary rules of procedure, it, too, must presuppose metaphysics in some sense. We would ask a question: Who is it in, say, the history of Judaism or Christianity, that has demonstrated the impossibility of metaphysical truth in terms of theology?

We would suggest that the rejection of all metaphysical truth by a critic is really nothing more than an attitude. Metaphysics is only abandoned, not refuted, by an act of *positing* one or more propositions for which there is no attempt to obtain evidence. Such an act is an act of will, not intellect. It is the way of ideologizing, not philosophizing.

THE APPLICATION OF THE FOUR CRITERIA TO THE HISTORY OF PHILOSOPHY

What is it in history that best measures up to the four criteria of metaphysics as a science? Can we turn to the writings of any one philosopher and say that there, and only there, is metaphysics as a science? No. For the writings, however systematic, of any one person are frozen in their incompleteness. But one of the criteria is that while metaphysics as a science must be systematic, the system must be open at one end and cannot be closed. And the system of any one man, confined as it is to his writings, is finished and closed. If metaphysics were identified with such a system, then it, too, would be finished. The future of metaphysics would reduce to a peculiar and sterile type of historicism in which no longer is the world studied but rather the writings of the master, which writings are approached in a manner similar to a Moslem making a textual exegesis of the Koran.

It would seem, then, that what must measure up to the four criteria is a developing system to which many philosophers have made contributions, although it may be that some one philosopher is more outstanding than others because of the adequacy and depth of his analysis and exposition. We would suggest that what best meets the test of metaphysics as a science is the classical realistic tradition, or, to be more exact, what is sometimes called "moderate realism," the system that has had a development from Aristotle through St. Thomas to the present. An alternative label is "Thomism"—one which, however, can be very misleading to the innocent.[6] We have suggested that moderate realism best measures up to what metaphysics is as a science. What is the evidence? Well, one may see now that it is so, in an intuitive manner. Or, better, one could apply the criteria in detail to moderate realism. But even that would not be sufficient, for "best" implies comparison, and it would be necessary to show that no other rival system is better. This is a negative approach through elimination. But it is perhaps somewhat fruitful, and in the limited time we have it will be the one we shall take. And there are many other questions. How do all of the other philosophers fit into the picture? What is to be said of idealism, naturalism, materialism, positivism, pragmatism, etc.? And is not Platonism also realism? We shall give a hint, in rather broad outline, of how these questions may be answered.

Pragmatism and positivism present no problems, for they do not pretend to be metaphysical systems. Pragmatism is a variant of either idealism or naturalism, and positivism is by definition anti-metaphysical.

Platonism. If moderate realism measures up best to being metaphysics as a science, it is still possible for a rival tradition to measure up *relatively* well or badly. The Platonic tradition would measure up relatively well, but would suffer when appraised in terms of the criterion of adequacy. The adequacy of Platonism is questionable because of the confusion of mental and real being when ideas or universals are considered to be independent of the mind, and hence require a separate realm for their locus. The critic may quickly point out that our use of the term "Platonism" is unclear, and that the term covers several different thought-strains in history. Furthermore, are we not begging the question and judging Platonism, or what is sometimes called "extreme realism," in terms of moderate realism rather than in terms of the four criteria? In reply we suggest that the fact of the various thought-strains helps to confirm rather than refute our thesis as to its relative inadequacy. Second, we mean to judge Platonism in terms of the criteria, and we believe that it can be shown to be relatively inadequate. However, since the issue here is the relative adequacy of two forms of realism, the problem is not quite as simple as we make it appear. Let us grant that it is debatable, and move on to less uncertain applications.

Idealism. Idealism and naturalism or materialism come naturally to mind when we think of possible alternatives to classical realism. Now, however ambiguous the term "idealism" may be, either it refers to something compatible with realism, or it does not. In the first case, idealism

refers to some variant of the Platonic realism we have already mentioned. On
the other hand, insofar as idealism is
something unique the reference is to certain strains of thought in modern philosophy, and we think of, say, Berkeley or
Kant or Hegel. The essence of modern
idealism has consisted in identifying
knowing and making or creating. Our
ideas or concepts are what we know, not
that by which we know. Idealism thus
fails to satisfy the criterion of autonomy,
for metaphysics no longer has any unique
formal object relative to other kinds of
knowledge. The nominalism of Berkeley
leads to Hume's skepticism. Kant, reduc-
ing knowing to making, tries to save positive science at the expense of metaphysics.
In order to overcome this philosophical
schizophrenia Hegel reduces knowing to
creating *ex nihilo*. In the name of metaphysical reason, metaphysics, as one autonomous kind of knowledge among others, is destroyed. Since it is a good exam-

ple of a system closed at both ends, there can be no development of Hegelianism, and hence it is condemned by the criterion of continuity. But if Hegelianism may be said to be the idealist version of the end of metaphysics, it can also be said to usher in the age of ideology.

Naturalism and materialism. In appearance, naturalism would seem to be a much more likely candidate for metaphysics as a science than would idealism. It certainly is ancient. And cannot there be said to be a development of it such that the four criteria are satisfied—at least, relatively well? A distinction must be made between ancient and modern naturalism. After allowances are made for the fact that we are dealing with a period in which metaphysics was potential and only beginning to emerge as systematic, that kinds of causes and kinds of knowledge were of necessity confused, nevertheless we can say that a naturalist such as, say, Democritus, was certainly a metaphysician and

a most important philosopher. A critic today can only follow the lead of Aristotle
and point out the relative inadequacy of
his thought, e.g., the confusion of a kind
of being with being itself, and the view of
causality as limited to the material and the
efficient. Democritus was not an ideologist. He sought truth about what he conceived being to be, even going so far as to
explain in terms of his atomism the nature
of that intuition whereby we see Reality
as it actually is, and not merely as it is
given to us in a distorted manner through
sense experience.

When we come to modern times the
picture is somewhat different. What does
it mean to return to a neo-Democritan
materialism after two thousand years of
development of realism? Was the motive
that of seeking metaphysical truth? It
might be charity as well as wisdom to
grant mixed motives in the beginning. But
in its development what has modern naturalism and materialism become? To

where do we turn to find it as even a pretended system of metaphysics? In its positivistic form naturalism is anti-metaphysical. If we turn to the dialectical materialism of the Marxists we find no metaphysics as a system, but rather an ideology. The time had come to cease interpreting the world; the problem was to change it. And for that purpose the concept of "matter" was and is a *weapon* against religion and what is called "idealism."

We find that the situation is no different when we turn to contemporary naturalism and materialism. In *Philosophy for the Future,* a volume in which a group of materialists state their position, we are told in the *Foreword* that "the materialist holds that philosophers cannot improve upon the descriptive concepts of matter supplied by the working scientist of his time."[7] In other words, "matter" is not even a metaphysical concept. When *used* outside of the physical sciences it can only be an "idea" in materialism as an ideology.

In another volume, *Naturalism and the Human Spirit,* a group of fifteen sum up naturalism as it stands at mid-century. Toward the end of the volume Mr. Costello, looking back on the essays, points out that the "new" naturalism has one liquidationist thesis, namely, that there is no supernatural and that God and immortality are myths. And then Mr. Costello adds: "I do not find any great unity, otherwise, among these new naturalists."[8]

A rather safe conclusion would seem to be this, that in terms of the four criteria modern naturalism and materialism, for the most part, are not so much inadequate metaphysical systems—they are not really metaphysics at all. Moreover, it would seem that this is no longer even a debatable issue. "Matter" and "method" (the "scientific method") are relevant to cognition only in the positive sciences. Otherwise, on a philosophical level, *they are only instruments for ideological strategy and have nothing to do with cognition or with metaphysics as a science.* We say that this is no longer debatable because this is something most naturalists and materialists insist upon. They do not confront the moderate realist with an alternative metaphysical system, they are not even talking about the same thing, they do not have the same purpose. Philosophically they only confront the realist with an "attitude" of being against him. Perhaps the time has come for realists to be realistic, to respect the wishes of naturalists and materialists, to take seriously their intentions which they have made very clear, namely, that their one unity is an attitude of aggression against all ontological truth, metaphysical or theological, as well as against any related subject, such as a non-relativistic Natural Law ethic, and that their weapon is ideology and not philosophy in their battle for institutional power.

By a process of elimination it appears that metaphysics as a science is to be found only in classical realism, and that the moderate realism of the Aristotle-Aquinas tradition can be considered the most adequate expression. At least, the burden of proof would seem to fall on one who would deny this. For, again, if metaphysics is a science, to where else do we turn? Does this mean that only realists, as defined, are metaphysicians? What of all the philosophers down through history who were not in the "true" tradition? Have they made no contributions? We can now only briefly indicate the nature of the answers.

Some modern philosophers. The history of philosophy is much broader than the history of moderate realism, for history must include all of the false and relatively inadequate alternatives in the development of metaphysics. Eliminate metaphysics in the history of philosophy and very little is left. If there is no metaphysical, and hence philosophical, truth, then there can be no history of philosophy.

There is only the history of ideas, or the history of the "intellectual" development of various persons. But if there is philosophical truth, then there is metaphysical truth. It exists and can be found in a relatively systematic form. If so, and "history" is to be taken in something more than its mere positive sense, then the history of philosophy will have to be interpreted in terms of metaphysics as a science, i.e., in terms of moderate realism. This means that the time has come when a sharp line must be drawn between the philosophers and the anti-philosophers, between philosophy and ideology, between the history of philosophy and the history of ideology, between the philosophy of history and an ideological view of history. It does *not* mean that some one, or a group, arrogantly, without evidence or reason, relegates to the limbo of anti-philosophy all those with whom there is disagreement. No one is to be relegated anywhere. It does mean that the time has come to respect the wishes of those who *freely will* not to be philosophers, who insist that there is no ontological, ethical, or logical truth, and that we recognize the *war* which they are waging against philosophy, often, in the name of philosophy.

An inadequate metaphysics is still metaphysics, and the proponent is a metaphysician, not an anti-philosopher. For example, Descartes, Spinoza, and Locke were philosophers, and from the standpoint of realism they made contributions to philosophy, although perhaps not in the way they suspected. From the standpoint of the history of philosophy, though not in intention, they demonstrated the philosophical blind alleys one can get into through confusing being with a mode of being. To metaphysics as a science their contribution was of value, but in a negative, not positive, way. Each one, because of the confusion mentioned, solved nothing, but rather created problems for succeeding generations. Finally, by inexorable logic, there came a time when thinkers had to say that if all this be metaphysics *as a science,* then there is no metaphysical truth. Do not the skeptic, the positivist, the pragmatist, and the Thomist all agree?

Was David Hume essentially a philosopher or an ideologist? He was a philosopher. Given the premises of Locke and Berkeley, that what we know are our ideas and that to be is to be perceived, Hume showed that the consequences land one in skepticism. And other things follow, too, such as reason being the slave of the passions. And who will disagree? This is philosophical analysis of a rather keen sort. It does not make of Hume an ideologist. Even from the standpoint of Hume's intention the most that can be said is that Hume, among others, established the philosophical foundations of ideology. But if, instead of rejecting the premises, a person accepts the conclusions of Hume, thus denying all metaphysical truth, and then uses his reason as a slave of his feelings in order to construct a world in idea to satisfy some practical purpose, then that person becomes an ideologist and not a philosopher.

Because of possible misunderstanding of the meaning of the four criteria and their application in the history of philosophy, the feelings of our non-Thomistic readers may require some assuagement at this point. Are we not saying that everyone, to be a philosopher today, must be a Thomist, or what we euphemistically call a "moderate realist"? Are we not advocating a restriction on the creative thinking of philosophers? Are teachers only to spoonfeed Thomism to students as if it were a kind of intellectual pablum? The answer to these questions is, no. What we are suggesting is a return to creative thinking and a turn away from ideology. Those of whom we are critical are precisely those who do spoonfeed Thomism. The parroting of Thomistic phrases, together with bad pedagogy, often obscures the truth of Thomism and hence strengthens the belief that it is a dead system incompatible with intellectual creativity, and that it has been sustained in apparent life only because of an authoritarian pronouncement of Pope Leo XIII. We would suggest that the only thing dead about Thomism is the way it is sometimes taught.

Existentialism. However, the critic pursues us. What are we to say about the apparently fruitful modern and contemporary developments in philosophy, e.g., phenomenology and existentialism. Well, let us see. Consider existentialism. Is a person an existentialist because he is emphasizing existence relative to essence, thereby correcting a tendency toward a metaphysical essentialism? If so, that is good; and it is metaphysics. Or, is the person's existentialism a substitute for metaphysics and/or theology? If so, this is quite different. He is a post-modern contemporary man, alienated from onto-

logical truth, both metaphysical and theological, and he finds himself in the crowd-
ed emptiness of cities, or in universities
with other rootless individuals. Being human, he can't stand it, and so he screams—
screams the only way an intellectual can
and yet keep away from those institutional
men in white gowns. He writes and ex-
presses his care and concern, his fear,
dread, and anxiety over the concrete existential situation in which he and others
find themselves. He speaks constantly of
encounter, and calls for commitment and
decision. To what? That is not clear. All
that is clear is that one must choose, one
must decide. And so, now, in the tradition
of those who first began the progressive
alienation from the true God, and who
could find only loyalty to loyalty, reverence for reverence, and faith in faith, he,
too—but now at the end of the process—
in desperation cries of his care about care,
his concern about concern; in agony he
dreads dread, fears fear, and is anxious

over anxiety; and in despair he commits
himself to commitment, and he makes a
decision to make decisions.

This is the outcrying of a sick soul, and
charity demands that he receive loving attention from those who are well. But his
writings prove nothing about, for, or
against metaphysics as a science, or moderate realism in particular. In fact, they
tell more about the psychology of the person than they do about existence or being.
His writings do not present metaphysical
truth along side of, or additional to, moderate realism. It just so happens that "anxiety" and "dread" are not metaphysical
categories, but rather those of the philosophy of human nature, a hybrid subject
resting in part upon metaphysics, or concepts relevant to religion and theology.
Furthermore, although metaphysics is
powerless to cure the sickness, it may help
to explain the cause. Historically speaking,
when man wrongly attempts to substitute
metaphysics for theology he may end up

trying to substitute psychology and personal biography for the metaphysics that has disappointed him. A rash of "personal philosophies of life" follow, and these are ideologies. In fact, the very notion of a "personal philosophy" is a contradiction, like "round square." For if it is to mean anything other than the tautology that any philosophical view is mine by virtue of the fact that I, as a person, have it, then it means that the philosophy is true because it is mine, personally. Of such stuff is nonsense made. Of course, truth must be grasped subjectively and made one's own. But the truth that is grasped must have its foundation in the "nature of things." Otherwise subjectivity merely grasps subjectivity, and the ego suffocates in its own embrace.

The critic may feel that we have missed the point completely, namely, that classical realism, in terms of the very criteria we have suggested is absolutely, not relatively, inadequate because it cannot take account of man's subjectivity; for is it not part of the essence of this system to reduce man, the subject, to an object? To correct this deficiency would require a substantial change necessitating the destruction of the system. Now this kind of criticism, if true, is a very serious one. The theoretical possibility of the truth of such criticism must be admitted. On the other hand, the criticism must have its evidence. However, what we find is not evidence, but a serious misunderstanding of realism.

In the first place, to consider man, the subject, as an object is not peculiar to Scholasticism or Thomistic realism. It is impossible to avoid it in any system of thought. It is tautological truth to say that if subjectivity is to become the object of thought, then it is the object of thought. If so, the criticism is irrelevant. Or, if it is relevant, it is against all metaphysics and philosophy, and not realism *as* philosophy.

In the second place, the understanding

of the individual person as subject is not the exclusive task of metaphysics. It is also the concern of natural law ethics, moral theology, psychology, law and jurisprudence, and even, in a sense, the novelist and the poet. Most important of all, it is the concern of religion. The Thomistic synthesis, on a philosophical level, can only do what it can *on that level*. Of course it does not deal adequately with such themes as conscience, guilt, choice, freedom, and death. But neither can any other philosophical alternative. It is no criticism of Thomism as philosophy that its adequacy extends only to philosophy. In fact, this is not only the Thomist's thesis, it must be anyone's thesis, that one kind of knowledge cannot be a substitute for another. Metaphysics, and other philosophical subjects based upon it, can only go so far in understanding the "I-Thou" relationship of a human person to God as Person, as well as the inter-subjective relations between human persons. For the most important truth philosophy must defer to religion and theology. This is a Thomistic thesis, and hence cannot be used as a criticism against it.

A third kind of radical criticism of moderate realism as not being able to account for the person as subject is based upon the interpretation of it as a closed system. Realism, says John Wild, attempts to be a science, and "the scientific mind . . . is outwardly directed toward objects of different kinds, and takes the observer and his existence for granted."[9] A new philosophy is needed for today. "Such a philosophy, if it is ever formulated, will differ from Greek thought and from Thomism in abandoning the claim to have demonstrated by a purely detached and objective reason . . . a system of thought that is in essence complete and closed."[10] The philosophy will be phenomenological in nature. After pointing out that many Catholic thinkers in Europe are working on such a philosophy and "are trying to find a place for [phenomenological developments] in the great Thomistic framework . . .," Mr. Wild continues, "In my opinion these attempts are doomed to failure. This synthesis has been outgrown. The history of philosophy has not ended."[11]

The answer to this kind of criticism has already been given in our analysis of the criterion of "system," where it was pointed out that moderate realism as a science is not a system closed at both ends and confined to the writings of St. Thomas. Such a caricature of Thomism is in fact based upon a confusion of the order of knowledge with that of learning and teaching. Sometimes Catholic teachers do present Thomistic realism in such a fashion that the appearance is given that it is a dead, closed system rather than a live, open one. But this is simply bad pedagogy, and had this been the point of Mr. Wild's criticism he would have shared a justifiable concern with many Catholic philosophers. However, it should be remarked that such a pedagogical mistake can only be made by a teacher who has some systematic philosophical truths to teach. Returning, now, to the order of knowledge, we suggest that a much more reasonable and fruitful position to take is that, for example, of Robert O. Johann who, aware of the same kind of problem as is Mr. Wild, tries to give "an explanation of the possibility of a philosophy of subjectivity as constituting a reasonable addition to the *philosophia perennis*, a certain broadening of its perspective, without amounting instead to a simple jettisoning of the thought and gains of centuries."[12]

Phenomenology. The term "phenomenology" as used is ambiguous. Insofar as it denotes a certain type of modern idealism, e.g., that of Husserl, then, in terms of the four criteria of metaphysics as a science, it must be appraised in the manner in which we have considered any kind of idealism. On the other hand, the term may refer to a method of pure description of

experience, without explanation or infer-
ence. If so, then, in the words of Harmon
M. Chapman, "the terms 'realism' and
'phenomenology' signify inseparable aspects of a single discipline."[13]

Linguistic Analysis. Analysis of language is as old as philosophy itself and
can be valuable as a metaphysical propae-
deutic. The question to be asked is: Does
a person indulge in linguistic analysis because he believes in metaphysical truth,
or because he doesn't? If the latter, then
such analysis is an attempt to show that
metaphysical sentences are not propositions because they are cognitively mean-
ingless. Since the limits of cognition can
never be determined by language analysis
alone, such a "view" reduces, like much of
modern naturalism, to an "attitude," that
of being against metaphysics. In itself
such a view is not an ideology, but rather
one of the many non-philosophical forms
of anti-philosophy, and probably would
not exist were it not for the fact that pro-

fessors of philosophy who no longer believe in philosophy must do something
if they are to continue to receive a salary
for doing that which they profess to be
impossible.

Some miscellaneous applications. It
should be clearly understood that the four
criteria we have considered are those for
metaphysics as a science. In the application of these criteria we have not meant
to disparage any honest search for metaphysical truth on the part of those philosophers who do not think of themselves
as in the classical realist tradition. Furthermore, there are many kinds of writings involving careful analysis, logical, historical and phenomenological, which make
a contribution to philosophical insight and
truth, and yet which are given by thinkers who are neither conscious of being
Thomistic realists, nor in fact are, and who
may in some ways be very much in op-
position. Hence, it is not really a paradox
to say that it is possible for a non-Thomist

realist to make a contribution to metaphysics as a science.[14]

Protestant Christian philosophy. Is there not a Protestant Christian philosophy? And if there is, may it not also measure up relatively well in terms of the four criteria? Although there have been various philosophies held by Protestants, it would be difficult to find any distinctive philosophy because Protestantism has tended to reflect the intellectual climate of each age. In the beginning it borrowed from Scholastic realism; later it was influenced by Kantian idealism. Today it tends to be either anti-metaphysical or positively ideological.

Exceptions, there are, of course, and one of the most important today is the development of a Protestant philosophy in Dutch Calvinism, e.g., the work of the philosopher, H. Dooyeweerd.[15] It aims to be realistic in a non-Thomistic sense. Whether there is any radical incompatibility with traditional realism is a matter

to be studied. It would seem that a "Reformed philosophy" is still in potency in
relation to the last four hundred years.
As Mr. William Young, himself a Calvin-
ist, remarks, in commenting on the development of Calvinism to the 19th century:
"At no point did Calvinism even display
the consciousness that in its theological
system were contained clues for the development of a radically unique system of
philosophy."[16]

CONCLUDING REMARKS

What we have tried to do is briefly to
clarify the philosophical *status quo*. First,
since both metaphysicians and ideologists
talk about being and similar matters, we
have suggested four criteria in terms of
which metaphysics as a science may be
distinguished from ideology. We agree
with the ideologist that much of what is
distinctive of modern philosophy is a rec-
ord of the failure to establish an alternative to the Thomistic synthesis, thus forc-

ing non-realists gradually into either skepticism or the ideological camp.

Second, since metaphysics and ideology
are, intellectually and otherwise, absolutely incompatible, it would be well for metaphysicians to avoid using the terms interchangeably and to recognize the distinction which the ideologist dare not admit.
Mr. Aiken, who favors ideology, says of
"metaphysical" answers: "Whether such
answers are 'cognitive' and 'true' or 'false'
in the scientific sense is unimportant.
What does matter is that the pictures of
reality which they present to us may en-
able us to organize our energies more adequately for the satisfaction of our total
needs as men. Then they will be 'true' in
the only sense of the term which is worth
considering."[17]   Presumably, what is the
case for metaphysics is *a fortiori* true for
logic, ethics, and other philosophical dis-
ciplines. Now, "human needs" is a question-begging term, for human needs in fact
define conflict. If ideas have only an in-

strumental function, then they remain eternally in conflict because there are no truths in terms of which human needs can be ordered. This is a "philosophy" of perpetual war under the guise of progressive humanism. It is a pure nihilism—intellectually the offspring of skepticism, which in turn is the grandchild of nominalism.

However, chaos can only be known in relation to order. Hence, although there is a philosophical foundation of ideology, there can be no ideological foundation of ideology. Herein lies the element of tragedy, for the ideologist can be what he is only so long as he is aware of the non-ideological truth against which, by his own admission, he must fight. If he admits the distinction between metaphysics and ideology, he condemns himself. If he does not admit it, he deceives himself. Of necessity he must prefer deception to condemnation. By the same necessity he must try to make this deception universal.

Third, if this be so, in this post-modern

era perhaps we should realize that the serious problem is not that of intellectual differences among philosophers seeking truth. Rather it is that of rival ideologists who seek alternative idea-weapons to destroy, through institutional control, the moral and religious heritage of the West. Between metaphysics as a cultural substructure and ideology as a cultural superstructure there is an infinite gap that can never be closed by our institutions through that magic of co-existence which confuses tolerance with indifference. A choice must be made.

A choice must be made, but in order to avoid misunderstanding we wish to emphasize that our thesis does not mean to imply restriction on the freedom of the thinker. If the application of the four criteria of metaphysics as a science to the history of philosophy has been correct, then it would seem that a serious metaphysician today must at least come to terms with moderate realism. This responsibility still allows him the utmost freedom. He may, if he so wishes, attempt a radical critique of Thomistic realism in the hope that his beginnings may in the future result in an alternative scientific metaphysics even more adequate. Whether successful or not, at least he prevents the Thomist from becoming smug and complacent. However, he is still faced with the fact that a potential metaphysics is not as yet a live alternative to an actual one, namely, the twenty-five hundred years of realism.

Ideologies exist, and probably always will exist. What we are suggesting is an increased awareness of the fact, thus respecting the wishes and freedom of the ideologist. If, as a Christian, I tell a person that there is only Heaven, and that he cannot freely will to go to Hell because there is no such place to go, then, although I may pleasantly confuse him, I am also restricting his freedom by eliminating alternatives. Likewise, if I, as a philosopher and metaphysician, refuse to admit the existence of ideology, and insist that all of those usually classified as philosophers in the history of philosophy are really philosophers, that they are all really seeking truth—even the truth about truth—whenever they use ontological terms, that we are all bursting with good will and rationality in trying to do the same thing, differing only in degree of insight and in the nature of our honest "mistakes," then I am not respecting the person and freedom of the ideologist, for I am refusing to take him seriously.[18]

On the other hand—and, once again, in order that there be freedom of choice— the metaphysician must reject the notion that all ontology is really only ideology. Theologically, especially in the United States, this often takes a neo-Feuerbachian form, resting on two assumptions: (1) God does not exist, but we may fruitfully use the terms referring to the divine attributes; (2) Atheism is the secret of religion. Now, it is true that there are non-theistic religions, and also that some "theologies" are ideologies. However, when he applies this to Christianity the ideologist is not taking theism seriously, with the result that we have forced upon us such a linguistically Orwellian reversal as "naturalistic theism"—a term which undoubtedly has use-value in institutional war, but has no more cognitive meaning than "round square" or "rope of dry sand."[19]

Since such deception is intrinsic to ideology, and by its own definition cannot be overcome, the most the metaphysician can do is to point it out.

Concomitant with this "religious" development there has existed a philosophical analogue which can be summed up in two statements: (1) Metaphysics does not exist, but metaphysical terms may be fruitfully used; (2) Ideology is the secret of metaphysics.

However, if this be not so, then there

is both metaphysics *and* ideology. We
have tried to show how they may be distinguished.

NOTES

1. Karl Mannheim, *Ideology and Utopia* (New York: Harcourt, Brace and Co., 1936), pp. 87, 268.

   Mannheim says: "Indeed we may say that for modern man pragmatism has, so to speak, become in some respects, the inevitable and appropriate outlook, and that philosophy in this case has simply appropriated this outlook and from it procceded to its logical conclusion." (p. 65) The conclusion is, of course, that all ontology is really ideological. Since this proposition is not an ontological proposition, but one about "knowledge," then pragmatism must be accepted by the ideologist as a true philosophical statement about human knowledge. Hence, pragmatism is not itself an ideology, but rather is the philosophical foundation of ideology. This is a rather embarrassing position, for the ideological notion of ontological "truth" presupposes a non-ideological notion of truth about the nature of knowledge.

2. Henry D. Aiken, *The Age of Ideology* (New York: The New American Library, 1956), p. 26.

3. *Ibid.*, p. 25.

4. *Ibid.*, p. 24. The ideologists referred to are those in the history of Western philosophy. In what follows we shall also be referring to metaphysics in the same historical tradition. The problem of Oriental philosophies is a separate matter, the considering of which, we believe, would require an addition to, but not an alteration of, our present analysis.

5. Wm. Oliver Martin, *The Order and Integration of Knowledge* (Ann Arbor: The University of Michigan Press, 1957).

6. The reference is, of course, to Thomism on the level of reason, not of faith. It may seem that we have constructed the four criteria in terms of Thomism and then "discovered" that it best satisfies them—a question-begging procedure. This raises the question of which is ultimate. The critic's case would be strongest if he could show that some non-realistic metaphysics best measures up to an alternative and more adequate set of criteria which is independent of that metaphysics.

7. R. W. Sellars, V. J. McGill, and M. Farber, (eds.), (New York: Macmillan, 1949), p. vii.

8. Y. H. Krikorian, (ed.), (New York: Columbia University Press, 1944), pp. 295, 296.

9. John Wild, "Can Christian Philosophy be Taught in a Christian College," *Philosophical Unity in the Educational Process,* (Publication of Christ the King Foundation of the Protestant Episcopal Church, 620 Barton Place, Evanston, Illinois, 1958), p. 31.

10. *Ibid.,* p. 28.

11. *Ibid.,* p. 37. In this article Mr. Wild sometimes confuses the order of learning and teaching with the order of knowledge. He is sensitive to the fact that so often Thomistic realism is presented as a dead and lifeless subject to the student, having little relevance to his life and to the present, concrete human world. He insists that there must be "teaching through living dialogue . . . " (p. 30). Not only is Mr. Wild quite correct here, but he shares this concern with many Catholic philosophers. However, from the fact that Thomistic realism is often presented in teaching as if the history of philosophy were closed, it does not follow that in the order of knowledge it must be rejected.

Another reason given for its rejection is that realism "is closed to the critical movements of modern thought." (p. 37) It is not clear to what he refers, and which would demand that he repudiate completely all of his mature thought as a contemporary realist. Since as late as 1953 he was a leader in the development of the "Realist Platform" (John Wild, (ed.), *The Return to Reason.* [Chiago, Henry Regnery Co., 1953], pp. 357-363), the "movements" to which he refers must have existed previously, the significance of which he was unaware. At any rate, Mr. Wild insists that a radically new philosophy is necessary, that we must reject such notions as "the timeless essence of man" and "a timeless truth" and resign ourselves "only to a human truth that grows and declines with history . . . " (pp. 38-39). It is to be hoped that Mr. Wild will soon clarify the nature of the evidence he professes to have found, and which would require the repudiation, in essentials, of the realism of which he was once a brilliant exponent.

12. Robert O. Johann, "Subjectivity," *The Review of Metaphysics,* XII, No. 2, 200.

This article is a good example of a realist

attempting to correct what some would say are deficiencies in traditional realism.

In this connection we may speak briefly to a related problem. The question may be raised: Is not the Socratic-Augustinian tradition quite as important as that of Aristotle-Aquinas? This is not the place to give an easy answer. But we shall make a few remarks, and in doing so we assume the question is genuine and not one of the type raised by those whose chief interest in Augustinianism is as a weapon against Thomism. First, there is a question of fact. Is there such a philosophy, of equal generality and breadth of synthesis, and analysis in detail, as to be compared to Thomistic realism? If not, then the tradition is one of emphasis in the history of realism.

For example, Dom Mark Pontifex, who leans toward Augustinianism, is highly critical of the usual Thomistic real distinction between essence and existence and develops this thesis: "There is a real distinction between creature and Creator, but not a real objective distinction between essence and existence in the dependent thing." (Dom Mark Pontifex and Dom I. Trethowan, *The Meaning of Existence,* [New York: Longmans, Green and Co., 1953], p. 74). Now, whereas Mr. Wild, in the light of this (*op. cit.*, p. 39) and other considerations, is prepared to separate himself from realism, Dom Pontifex points out: "I submit that nothing really fundamental to Thomism is rejected in this theory . . ." (*op. cit.*, p. 75). He says, further: "It would certainly be unthomist in spirit to treat the letter of St. Thomas' text as the final criterion." (*ibid.*, p. 73). If Thomistic realism is not falsely interpreted as a closed system wholly identified with a group of writings, there would seem to be little reason to think of the Socratic-Augustinian tradition as a rival—certainly not on the level of metaphysics as a science.

13. Harmon M. Chapman, "Realism and Phenomenology," John Wild, (ed.), in *The Return to Reason*, (Chicago: Henry Regnery Co., 1953), p. 3.

14. The work of Paul Weiss (cf. *Modes of Being* [Carbondale, Ill.: Southern Illinois University Press, 1958]) would undoubtedly be in the realistic tradition. Although Thomists may find disagreements, it is a work that merits study.

15. H. De Jongste, David H. Freeman, and William Young (trans.), *A New Critique of Theoretical Thought* (3 vols.; Philadelphia: The Presbyterian and Reformed Publishing Co., 1955). To my knowledge there is no Protestant philosophy in the United States or Canada comparable to this work. It raises again the old question as to whether there is such a thing as a Protestant or Catholic philosophy. With respect to realism two positions might be taken.

(1) Dooyeweerd's work is realism, but outside of the Thomistic tradition. Certainly the author intends this.

(2) In essence it is compatible with Thomism if the latter is not interpreted in an essentialistic fashion. This might plausibly be defended by showing that, analogous to the transformation equations for changing polar to cartesian coordinates, in spite of differences in terminology there are more philosophical equivalents than not.

16. William Young, *Toward a Reformed Philosophy* (Grand Rapids: Piet Hein Publishers, 1952), p. 35.

17. Henry D. Aiken, *The Age of Ideology*

(New York: The New American Library, 1956), p. 270.

18. Of course there is always a danger in judging that someone lacks good will or is irrational. But the risk must be taken. This view would seem to be challenged by Mr. R. L. Barber who, in a very interesting article, says that with respect to the history of philosophy we must assume "the moral earnestness and intellectual competence of the thinkers who have devised and bequeathed the great majority of these systems." ("Philosophic Disagreement and the Study of Philosophy," *Tulane Studies in Philosophy,* vii [1958], p. 27.) However, Mr. Barber does not make the distinctions between philosophers, anti-philosophers, and ideologists. To the former his article is relevant. I do not know how he would handle the case of the "moral" earnestness of one who denies the possibility of all moral truth.

19. In the "brave new world" even a positivist will be a reactionary, for he merely denies metaphysics. What will be required is its "reduction." Metaphysical "propositions" have been reduced to those of mathematics, physics,

etc. An historian, Mr. R. G. Collingwood "gets into the act," too, by "showing" that all metaphysical propositions are really historical propositions. (*An Essay on Metaphysics,* [London: Oxford University Press, 1948]). Hence, he can say: "If 'God exists' means 'somebody believes that God exists' (which it must mean if it is a metaphysical proposition) it is capable of proof. The proof must of course be an historical proof, and the evidence on which it is based will be certain ways in which this 'somebody' thinks." (p. 188) We are informed that "the Christian Church has always taught that metaphysics is an historical science." (p. 188)

The Aquinas Lectures

Published by the Marquette University Press,
Milwaukee 3, Wisconsin

St. *Thomas and the Life of Learning* (1937) by
the late Fr. John F. McCormick, S.J., professor of philosophy, Loyola University.

St. *Thomas and the Gentiles* (1938) by Morti-
mer J. Adler, Ph.D., director of the Institute
of Philosophical Research, San Francisco,
Calif.

St. *Thomas and the Greeks* (1939) by Anton C.
Pegis, Ph.D., former president and present
professor of the Pontifical Institute of Mediaeval Studies, Toronto.

The Nature and Functions of Authority (1940)
by Yves Simon, Ph.D., professor of philosophy of social thought, University of Chicago.

St. *Thomas and Analogy* (1941) by Fr. Gerald
B. Phelan, Ph.D., professor of philosophy, St.
Michael's College, Toronto.

St. *Thomas and the Problem of Evil* (1942) by
Jacques Maritain, Ph.D., professor *emeritus*
of philosophy, Princeton University.

Humanism and Theology (1943) by Werner Jaeger, Ph.D., Litt.D., University professor, Harvard University.

The Nature and Origins of Scientism (1944) by John Wellmuth.

Cicero in the Courtroom of St. Thomas Aquinas (1945) by the late E. K. Rand, Ph.D., Litt.D., LL.D., Pope professor of Latin, *emeritus*, Harvard University.

St. Thomas and Epistemology (1946) by Fr. Louis-Marie Regis, O.P., Th.L., Ph.D., director of the Albert the Great Institute of Mediaeval Studies, University of Montreal.

St. Thomas and the Greek Moralists (1947, Spring) by Vernon J. Bourke, Ph.D., professor of philosophy, St. Louis University, St. Louis, Missouri.

History of Philosophy and Philosophical Education (1947, Fall) by Étienne Gilson of the *Académie française*, director of studies and professor of the history of Mediaeval philosophy, Pontifical Institute of Mediaeval Studies, Toronto.

The Natural Desire for God (1948) by Fr. William R. O'Connor, S.T.L., Ph.D., former professor of dogmatic theology, St. Joseph's Seminary, Dunwoodie, N.Y.

St. Thomas and the World State (1949) by Robert M. Hutchins, former Chancellor of the University of Chicago.

Method in Metaphysics (1950) by Fr. Robert J. Henle, S.J., dean of the graduate school, St. Louis University, St. Louis, Missouri.

Wisdom and Love in St. Thomas Aquinas (1951) by Étienne Gilson of the *Académie française*, director of studies and professor of the history of Mediaeval philosophy, Pontifical Institute of Mediaeval Studies, Toronto.

The Good in Existential Metaphysics (1952) by Elizabeth G. Salmon, associate professor of philosophy in the graduate school, Fordham University.

St. Thomas and the Object of Geometry (1953) by Vincent Edward Smith, Ph.D., professor of philosophy, University of Notre Dame.

Realism and Nominalism Revisited (1954) by Henry Veatch, Ph.D., professor of philosophy, Indiana University.

Imprudence in St. Thomas Aquinas (1955) by Charles J. O'Neil, Ph.D., professor of philosophy, Marquette University.

The Truth That Frees (1956) by Fr. Gerard Smith, S.J., Ph.D., professor and chairman of the department of philosophy, Marquette University.

St. Thomas and the Future of Metaphysics (1957) by Fr. Joseph Owens, C.Ss.R., associate professor of philosophy, Pontifical Institute of Mediaeval Studies, Toronto.

Thomas and the Physics of 1958: A Confrontation (1958) by Henry Margenau, Ph.D., Eugene Higgins professor of physics and natural philosophy, Yale University.

Metaphysics and Ideology (1959) by Wm. Oliver Martin, professor of philosophy, University of Rhode Island.

Uniform format, cover and binding.